You are the people.
You are this season's people—
There are no other people this season.
If you blow it, it's blown.

"If not you, who?
If not now, when?"
   —Hillel

PUBLISHER   Paul Mandelstein   EDITORS   Matthew McClure
Philip Schweitzer   Rachel Sythe   Cornelia Mandelstein   Edine
Frohman   Ellen Schweitzer   William Meyers   Rita Sherman
ART   Mark Schlichting   Peter Hoyt   Nancy Leffer   James
Hartman   Alan   Bishop   Edith   Powell   Gregory   Lowry
Mary   Wheeler   PHOTOGRAPHY   Daniel   Luna   Clifford
Chappell   David   Frohman   Valerie   Epstein   Lisa   Griffin
Mary   Felber   Gary   McLaughlin   Peter   Schweitzer   Camille
Vaughn   Rick Smolan   Jean-Pierre Laffond / Sygma (Mother Teresa
photo)   PRINTING   Robert   Seidenspinner   Alan   Meltzer
Bernard   Cohen   John   Seward   Malcolm   White   Steven
Wasserman   Andrew   Nestler   Frank   Michael   Michael
Tassone   LITHOGRAPHY   Jeffrey   Clark   COMPOSING
Jane   Johnson   Catherine   Ridenour   Julia   Russell   Carolyn
James   LAYOUT   Katherine   Hotaling   Sheila   Lawyer
Kathryn McClure   RECORDING   Jean Kahan   TRANSCRIPTS
Ellen   Brothers   Betsy Van Camp   Susan Goldberg   Debbie
Maligno   Marty Branch   Sylvia Anderson   SALES   Bruce
Moore   Judd Hoffman   Jane Hunnicutt   Stephanie   Blevins
Jim Bernard   ©1976 The Book Publishing Company, The Farm,
Summertown, Tennessee 38483.   ISBN Number 0-913990-05-1.   For
permission to reprint, contact The Farm.

...this season's people

a book of spiritual teachings by Stephen Gaskin

The Book Publishing Company — Summertown, Tennessee 38483

Life is like
stepping onto a boat
which is about to sail
out to sea   and sink.
suzuki roshi

Get your mind unbound and free; and then, from the loosest, highest, best place you have, with the fastest and most humorous mind you can get together, you can reach out and make a try at understanding Spirit.

It's so subtle that you have to be quick: you can't have been thinking of yourself. It passes in the blink of an eye.

There is a plane of experience, other than the three-dimensional material plane, which can be felt by a human being. Many religions tell of people experiencing that plane — the stories of miracles and visions and revelations. There is much religious teaching telling us how to get to that plane.

It is a plane of experience that many thousands of people in this generation were catapulted into through the psychedelic revolution. There are still people all over the country saying, "Wow, what was *that?*"

The only thing that can answer that question is an understanding of the spiritual plane — understanding the nature of the relationship of man to the Universe, understanding that human beings are telepathic.

If people never get above the purely signal level of communication, and don't become telepathic, they haven't explored their full human birthright. Telepathy is a high and Holy thing.

When a bunch of people experience it together — when they really feel each other's presence and the presence of the Holy Spirit, they call it Holy Communion.

You can't understand God.
You can't define God,
and you can't contain God.

But you can, if you don't look at yourself, *be* God.

The way to keep from looking at yourself is to be so busy doing your best that you don't have anything left over to look with.

You can't know the totality of God with your finite mind, because God is infinite, and your material plane intelligence is finite—it cannot contain an infinite thing. But if you aren't pressing about the totality, and just relax and observe what's in front of you, you are knowing God, because that's all there is to know.

There is nothing else to know; and the knowledge, the knower, the thing known, and the act of knowing *are all one* and *are all God.*

You are the eyes with which God looks, and the mind through which God understands itself.

But if you've thought of the Deity as something easy to understand, that isn't true. The Deity is huge. It is larger than your mind can encompass, and it disappears in every direction infinitely. It's very hard to put any personality on something that disappeared off into the distance the last time you were searching, so you couldn't know whether you were looking at a tenth of it, or a hundredth of it, or a millionth of it. All you know is that it disappeared when you were last looking.

The Universe is a vibratory entity, and you can affect the vibrations one way or another by what you do. Everything has vibrations. Colors are vibrations, sounds are vibrations; so is concrete. So is thought. So is the Universe, God — all vibrations.* And if that's what it's all made out of, then you have a technology for learning how to deal with vibrations.

Non-space/time doesn't have any personality. It doesn't have any differentiated beings. It doesn't have any separateness of entities. Those are all space/time functions. It does have a clear set of vibrations and rules of its own which are just as real and just as reliable as the fact that something falls 32 feet per second per second. If you behave in certain ways in the material plane, you will resonate with certain of those vibrations from the nonmaterial plane.

*Since there is no space to vibrate in and no time to measure rate of vibrations in the spiritual plane, let it be known that "vibration" is a figure of speech.

If you resonate a vibration that is very high—

love   everybody,
                    willing-to-lay-your-life-on-the-
line-for-mankind,
                    we're-all-in-it-together,
                                        no-
body's-going-to-live-off-of-anybody

—you are going to resonate that pure vibration out of the non-space/time place that we call Christ Consciousness, or the Consciousness of the intermediary between God and man.

We are all parts of God. Each one of us has an electrical body field that surrounds us, and a mind field that goes on to Infinity. Whenever you have two electrical fields together, there is another field that exists that is the vector-resultant of those fields. And no matter how many fields you have together, there is always present a vector-resultant group vibration that everyone partakes of. That vibration is *more than the sum of its parts: the totality of all our vibrations go together to make that one pure vibration which is God.*

Religion is something that lives in the hearts of the people. We honor the old religions, like Buddhism and Christianity and Judaism and Islam, because they're enshrinements of a heavy thing that happened in the hearts of a certain generation. There are spiritual levels of experience that man is heir to. In times when there's a lot of material success in the world, folks sometimes forget to tune into these fine things and lose the knack, maybe for generations at a time. And whenever it comes back, it's always a big flash.

There is something happening now that doesn't have a name on it because it isn't old enough to have a name; but it's living in the hearts of the people.

If you but know it, in your highest and your finest and your most honest places in your own heart, *God is speaking to you*. Even now. All the time, in your highest and finest places.

It is not complicated or unusual or weird to know what God wants: If God is God at all, He wants justice and freedom and health and happiness and equality for everyone. If you know that's what God really wants, you'll help out along those lines.

Here are the keys to Heaven:

LOVE GOD.

And here are the keys to hell: "Well, I know I got

LOVE YOUR NEIGHBOR
AS YOURSELF.

take care of everybody, but I just want to get a little for myself first."

For a few years, I had been hearing interesting noise from people like Aldous Huxley and William James: *There are other levels of experience, separated from ordinary consciousness by the filmiest of veils.*

I could say, "Well, that's subjective. There's no way you can prove it." It was the old philosophical problem: How do you know what you know? Then I ran across a weird phenomenon. Somebody, talking about it just as though it were ordinary, said: *And another strange thing about psychedelics is the phenomenon of the contact high. The contact high is a phenomenon by which someone who has* **not** *ingested a psychedelic substance but who is in contact with someone who has, will also get high.*

That ran past all my carefully ordered cosmology, and I said, "*What!?* You say *what!?* Does Dr. Rhine know this? What is this thing that passes between these people?" It implied that there is some kind of medium that exists between people, and that the very phenomenon of *stonedness* can be sent as a telepathic message.

I explored this thing for months and months with my friends. We checked it out for a couple of years. We would say, "Did you feel what I felt when I felt that, or was I just having a subjective experience that you weren't in on?" If you were going to check out something like that, wouldn't you want to be careful? Wouldn't you want to be sure you weren't only fooling yourself?

Then we got the idea that it was *really there,* and we began to feel like we were at the beginning of the discovery of a new territory— like the people who put the Constitution together for this country, saying, "Here's a whole new territory. We have to find some ground rules." We started thinking, *What are the ground rules? What is the etiquette of a telepathic society?* How does one order one's mind when you live in a Universe where there is not a wall around your head, where your skull is not the limit of your consciousness, but that you actually share space with other people—*that you interpenetrate.* What is the etiquette? What is the political science when we can all be in the same place at the same time?

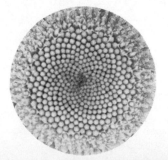

We started considering the assumptions behind that, and discovered that many of them had already been thought up. We found that many of the assumptions we were searching for were already in use in religion.

We found out that mankind has known that mankind is telepathic for thousands and thousands of years, and that it's so pure and so delicate a thing to bring about that they call it *Holy*. You have to *clean your heart*. If you want to communicate with people at that level, you can't have an impure thought about them. It muddies it up and makes it so unclear that you can't communicate. We found that you have to *really try* to be pure in your heart to experience Holiness.

The practice of real love and impeccable correctness and politeness and care among each other is only the beginning stage of the kind of peaceful society in which you may talk seriously about spiritual enlightenment.

What we expect is to be truthful; to be kind; to try to share; to try to love one another. Some folks don't recognize that as a discipline: They say, "Oh, that old stuff. . ." And it may not sound too difficult, unless you've ever tried it. But if you ever try it, you'll know it's an exacting discipline.

I know something. I know we're all One.
I know it so well that if I'm falling out of a tree,
I know we're all One before I hit the ground.
I'm not going to forget it; I can't give it up.

In the light of planetary communication and the current state of the world, we have to recognize that other cultures have had their planetary spiritual teachers. We can't be in an exclusive position in regard to the rest of mankind, because it is vitally important that we evolve some common philosophical religious assumptions—in order that mankind may survive. Without them, there's a good chance we won't.

It is of paramount importance to recognize that God is One. There are a lot of differences among the religions at lower levels. At the highest level, they become One.

The mystical sect of Christianity is called the Gnostics. Buddhism has Zen. Hinduism has the yogis. Judaism has the Hassidim. The Moslems have the Sufis. If you study their writings, you will discover that they talk again and again and again about exactly the same phenomena, the same experiences, the same realizations. They've obviously been to the same territory. There are certain realms of the mind that, if man ventures into them, it changes him, and he comes back different.

Religion only seems different if you're dealing with a retailer. If you deal with a wholesaler, they all get it from the same distributor.

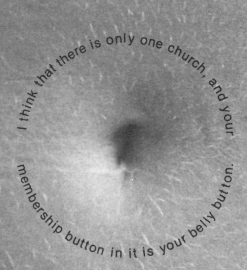

I think that there is only one church, and your membership button in it is your belly button.

In the religious revival that's happening in the country now, we're beginning to see that real live human values, nonconceptual, compassionate, and real, are more important than social standing, money, or any of that. If you're not straight with your fellow monkeys, then being chairman of the board doesn't help you out.

Religion is a *generic* term for how we relate to our Universe and how God and our Universe relate to us, and what is our proper relationship and perspective in the Universe.

There shouldn't be anything deeper than your religion. Your religion is how you really get along with folks — not what you may claim your religion is.

Your religion ought to make a difference to you in your daily life; it ought to make it easier for you, not in the sense that you don't have to try, but that it *makes sense for you*. If you're not getting along with your kid, it ought to help you out with your kid. It ought to help you out during childbirth; it ought to help you during the death of somebody who's close to you. It ought to help you through the heavy passages in life.

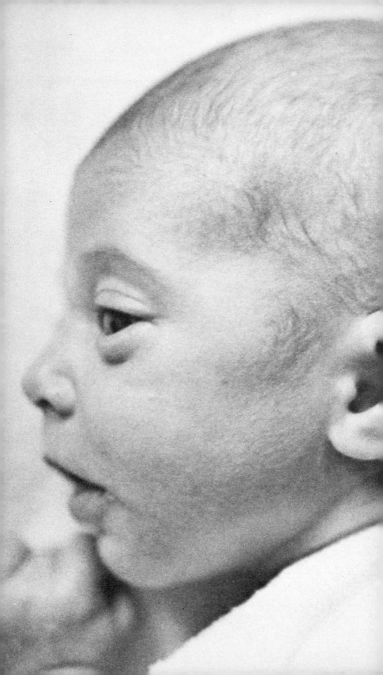

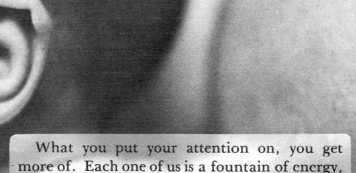

ATTENTION IS ENERGY

What you put your attention on, you get more of. Each one of us is a fountain of energy, a valve through which universal life energy is metered into the world, and we can each point our self at whatever we want to. We add life force to our surroundings—to everything we pay attention to. If you put your attention on the best, highest, finest, most beautiful thing that you can, *that* will be amplified.

Keep your attention in the here-and-now. Don't past-trip. Putting your attention in the past means that here-and-now is continuing on without you. The more time you spend in the past, the farther and farther out of register you are.

Don't put your attention into the future, other than a reasonable amount of plans which you intend to carry out. Putting your attention out into the future is like when a squirrel runs out on a tree limb—when he gets way out into the small limbs, it gets very shaky. When you get out into the thin possibilities, it gets very unlikely and it tends to get you paranoid.

So tripping in the past gets you schizophrenic, and tripping in the future tends to get you paranoid. Hang out in the here-and-now. It is healing. When you're in the here-and-now, accept it as reality. Don't think about it or run it through your mind-filter when it's coming in. Accept it.

A meditative state is pure perception: not being conceptual about the here-and-now. That's what most Zen discipline is about: not past-tripping, not future-tripping, and not being conceptual in the here-and-now.

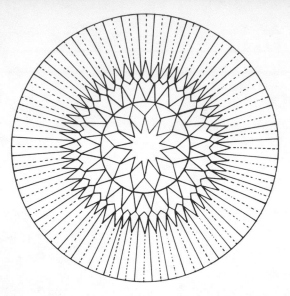

One of the things that teachers of meditation are trying to teach you is to be able to put your attention where you want it, and to follow out a difficult idea. I don't think that some people are smarter than others; I think that some people are willing to put more effort into following an idea.

Within each one of us is a spark of God. Some people call it inborn intelligence: a capacity to look out and see something. That capacity is so strong that if you look at someone and you see something in them that you like, you don't have to say anything, or give them a bouquet or write them a poem or send them a card. *If you just see something in them that you like, that thing will become stronger and it will come out at you; and they will do it more for you.*

Everybody needs attention—it's a human requirement, just like oxygen and water. The need for it begins as soon as we're born, and if we don't get it in a fair way, we'll learn outlaw habits of getting it. People will do outrageous things to get attention, because it is life force and energy. The reason to be discriminating about what you give your attention to, is to give real help to a person. That's how we all be each other's teachers: what we dig in each other, we reinforce.

Paying attention to what we choose to pay it to is probably the greatest freedom we have.

We all control what happens in the future by what we pay attention to in the present. If you perceive it to be improving and a groove, it improves and is a groove.

If you see that something should be a way, assume it's going to be that way.

The Nazz, stompin' on a sweet, swingin' beat, goin' down the road. The Nazz talkin' 'bout

**How pretty the flowers,
how pretty the hours,
how pretty me, how pretty you,
how pretty he, how pretty she.**

Nazz had them pretty eyes. He wanted everybody to see through his eyes so they could see how pretty it was.

—Lord Buckley

In Zen, they say you should world, instead of leaving it. because the distraction

learn to interact with the
Incorporate the distraction,
is also Buddha.

The more agreement there is about putting your attention into reality, the stronger and healthier everybody will be. It's better to pay attention to what *is*, because that's better mind food. A little attention to what is *not* is like spice for your mind food, to keep you from getting dull and not thinking anything new. But if you put *all* your attention into what is *not*, then your mind is going to get jaded and dull, and lose sensitivity to reality.

On the other hand, while you're soliding up your reality, you can't be so square as to make it so miracles don't work. You can't get so rigid you can't do miracles, can't do healings. You want your reality just loose enough that you can do a little miracle now and then. But not so loose that it starts getting chancy and problematical for the kids and the folks out on the fringes. It has to be good and solid for everybody.

—the question is
how quickly
can you forget
all that
and go on
to the next flash.

HELPING MAN IS A GOOD PLACE

TO START YOUR SEARCH FOR GOD

If you're not steering your mind, it's running on automatic pilot and goes a million times faster than you can steer it.

Rather than figuring it out, and saying, "Is this right?" or "Where would this be in the light of contemporary philosophy?"—that *first flash* is your best bet. I try to trust myself and trust myself until I can just move on that first flash. If we all moved together in our interaction on that first flash, we would be incredibly fast and smart. If every time you asked a question, the next thing that came back was the answer instead of "Huh?" or if they just said, "I don't know," and let you clear the circuit to do the next thing—if we just all answered honestly and correctly the first time, it would be so easy, so incredibly fast and smart—we would just be fabulous.

You have to learn to trust your mind—don't try to force it and push it in various ways. The more you trust it and the more you let it run on its automatic pilot, the faster and smarter and heavier it gets. It lets you out when you trust it. It's a good one—trust it.

Any time something is hard for you to do, bring yourself to bear; pay attention to it. Concentrate yourself. Come on to it with all your energy focused. That's all karate and breaking bricks is—

is having all your attention focused when you hit. You can break bricks if your attention is focused. If your attention is not focused and the swing is the same, you might break your hand.

Most of us walk around in whatever consciousness we're in, and we think that's it. We think that's all there is. If you ever get enough perspective to step outside yourself, and see someone else's viewpoint. . .I saw a young man consider, for the first time in his life, the possibility of someone else's viewpoint besides his own. During the time he was considering that, he became engulfed in three feet of white light. . .

One of the highest and Holiest religious experiences that is available to mankind is to get outside your head for a couple of seconds and realize that the sun doesn't rise and set in your armpit.

God is the center of the Universe, and we are all like rays extending out from God. When we act, it is God acting through us. When we have a new idea, it's God coming through us with that new idea.

I used to be very attached to thinking that I was having good ideas. Then, just for a second, I seriously thought about God coming through me—even in something like a good idea I thought I'd had, and Bang! I had this beautiful rush of spiritual energy that came on to me so strong and so sweet that I had to let go of everything I was doing and just lay back in my chair and relax and let these beautiful rays of spiritual energy come over me.

I found that I never really understood the Sermon on the Mount and the Beatitudes until I had experienced for myself what Jesus had seen. After I had seen the other level of experience for myself, it all made as absolutely perfect sense as, "If you're going to put this television set together, hook up wire A to terminal A, and if you don't wire it that way, it's going to blow up." It's just that clean.

I saw that Spirit was real, and I saw that karma mattered, and I saw that telepathy was real, and I saw that folks really did have communication from heart to heart and from soul to soul, and I saw that, contrary to modern psychology, *you can know your brother.*

Psychology teaches that communication is like taking a rock and wrapping a note around it and throwing it, and the other person catches the rock and unwraps it and reads the note. They say that's all you can know about somebody — and that's not true. *One person can know another person.* You can go to that place where you share souls and you can *know* somebody, and you are *not* alienated and you do *not* live in a box.

We are all really one thing, and we're all in this together, and no matter how we make it look, we are really and truly going to share fortunes. The sun is going to shine or not according to God's whim, as usual, and we'll share those fortunes.

There is an order of real experience that is, to some people, as real and common and everyday as whether the sun shines or whether it rains, or whether there's enough to eat. It can be as easily and plainly discernible as whether the lights are on or not; and the majority of the culture doesn't even believe in it — it has heard rumors out at the edges somewhere, that there is *something else* besides the meat part. It is a real religious experience.

In
San Francisco,
when heavy psychedelics
were at their peak, people were
seeing things three or four times a
week that one sight of it should have
gone *wham* and just straightened
them. They should have said, "Wow,
look at that," and just got cool right
then, but they were so jaded from
having done it a hundred times or two
hundred times that it didn't have any
juice. It was an example of, "If the
salt of the earth loses its savor,
wherewith shall you salt it?"
As familiar as religious experience may become to us, we
don't dare let it get
ordinary. This is called
keeping sacred things
sacred.

Your
intelligence
varies according to your
condition, your sanity, and
how much energy and Holy Spirit
you're able to get together — you
can change your intelligence and
you can get smarter.

Sometimes you realize something
that's so heavy and makes you so much
smarter on the spot that you realize
you just got smarter, and you notice
how dumb you were before. It's a
very humbling experience. It gets
you high, just because it gets
you so much smarter to
understand that. That
kind of heavy realiza-
tion can be called
kensho.

Some Hindus refer to the kind of energy that you keep on as *shakti*. They say you should guard your accumulation of shakti, and be careful with your energy, because whatever you let your energy out on is going to be furthered, whether it's a good cause or a bad cause: if you put your energy on it, it will make it prosper.

I try to be faithful to that energy, trying to conserve it so I'll have some if I need it. I don't need to have such a head of steam on that I'm just crackling and hallucinating every second. It's nice to do that once in a while, just to remind yourself that it does that. But I want to have enough energy on that if I run into somebody who's scared in the dark, I can say, "It's okay. It's not scary. I'm here, too, and I'm not scared."

any one of us by ourself.

Magicians studying will are learning to contain an immense amount of energy with their ego. The most energy that you can possibly contain with your ego is less than not having ego and being open to everybody else, because then you have access to everybody's energy — the Universe's energy — and it is so much more than anybody can possibly contain. Anybody who keeps their energy to themselves for a certain length of time gets stagnant, and they really need a little fresh water to come through. They may get a little irritable and a little dumb from getting stagnant. It's a helping and a healing if you can get them to open up and let a little clean stuff flow through their system. The real secret is: *The most energy you can have is uncontained.*

Sometimes you push very hard and you expend a lot of energy, and you get to where you don't have too much energy. You have to stop and relax and let yourself fill up. Maybe you're in a hurry, but it's more important to relax. You'll get so much smarter and more efficient. *It'll be worth the time you put into it—just stop and let everything out.*

Your stoned is just a little surplus of life force in your aura. If you aren't using it, give it to a kid, or give it to a plant or something. But don't just let it dissipate away. If you've got any juice, give it to somebody while you've got it. It's all you can do with it.

The way you learn how to have juice on is to get some juice on. "To those that have, shall be given."

You must be in a state of grace to receive grace.

If somebody isn't respectful of the energy, it makes it go down. *Be sacred.* Recognize that the Holy Spirit is there, and be respectful of it, and don't drive it away.

The thing that gives me the most peace is the feeling of *presence* — the telepathic awareness of my fellow man. You can feel it through your body, and you don't have to be with anyone to feel it. You can be by yourself, and just relax into that, because it's around us all the time. It's the Holy Spirit, always there to sustain us, inhabiting each one of us, indestructible and immortal.

There's plenty of energy. It's not like we lose energy or gain energy. It's there all the time.

You can look at your past actions and see that you have been fair and honest in all of your dealings with other people. If you haven't, you'll be uptight and it will cut down your energy. That's knowledge of good karma.

The most important thing to understand about life force energies is that *you can move them with your mind*. You can do real things—healing, teaching things.

"To see the universal and all-pervading Spirit of Truth face to face one must be able to love the meanest of creation as oneself. And a man who aspires after that cannot afford to keep out of any field of life. That is why my devotion to Truth has drawn me into the field of politics; and I can say without the slightest hesitation, and yet in all humility, that those who say that religion has nothing to do with politics do not know what religion means."

—Gandhi

The way you can stay high is by speaking truth: not only by doing good, but by speaking truth.

Everybody has been somewhere that's their benchmark for high; and if they're lucky, they'll never get down past the place where they'll forget that—even if they say they're not high right now, they can remember there was a place where they were high. When people get down so low that they forget they were high, that's like being in hell. You can make spiritual agreements with people to help each other stay high.

You can see right into people's souls. And if you can be compassionate and not revolted by anything you see, you can give people exact, unemotional information on the nature of their subconscious, and you can help them become more sane. Sometimes, when I'm talking to someone and telling them what I see in their head, I see them get prettier and better looking word by word as I tell them about it. If you can help somebody's subconscious be conscious, it's like bringing their soul out of hell. It's a heavy responsibility.

"The spirit of life relates to what has been described by the word "heaven"; the phenomenal world around us to what is described by the word "earth." Heaven and earth are one. Only man, in his foolishness, endeavors to separate them. To the extent that he is successful in this it becomes hell in his own experience. Hell is simply the absence of the experience of heaven; it is the absence of the experience of life, in whatever degree. The experience of life as it really is, is heaven."
—Lord Martin Cecil
in *Being Where You Are*

You have to use all your good judgment, and all your compassion, and courage, and tact, and taste, to say heavy things to people in ways that will be valuable to them, rather than just knocking them off their own center.

Sometimes a person can say the truth, but be doctrinaire about it, so it's a lie anyway. The truth, if said ignorantly, is not the truth. You have to know it's the truth when you say it, for it to be the truth.

You need to be truthful, and you need to be kind. You also need to be helpful, and your information has to be relevant.

If you're doing what's right, you'll know it. If not, don't fool yourself.

If you want to communicate with people, you have to work at it all the time, every waking minute. You have to work at it really hard, because many people are a little bit afraid.

If you think you've done enough when you do fifty per cent of the work, that won't make it, because to touch some people you may have to do a hundred per cent of the work. You can't ever say, "Well, I've tried hard enough." You have to keep on trying and keep on trying, remembering that folks really do want to be touched. They really do want to be communicated with.

Being spiritual does not mean to become as esoteric and as different as you possibly can, but to become like a solvent that can melt away the differences between people until only the essential thing is left. If we really understand what we're doing, we ought to get it on and find essential agreement with anybody.

Sometimes I have to watch stuff happen several times before I see the dynamics of the situation. But if I ever get a good grasp on what's really going on and who did what to whom and how they did it, I will not call off the meeting until I get that expressed and understood.

Sometimes I can't express it to the person involved, because he is too involved. I might just end up having to tell all the witnesses. Well, that's free will. If a person doesn't want to understand, he isn't going to. He will later, probably.

And you have to allow for folks to do that. You don't want to get so arbitrary with folks that it's an either/or situation where they have to split.

You can have the presence of mind, right in the middle of a hassle, to realize the other person probably doesn't want to be in it either.

If you can make a graceful place for him to get out, he'll want to get out of it. Give him a little room; don't put anybody in a corner—frequently, they'll figure it out and come back and say, "Hey, man, I was on a trip. I don't want to do that." Recognize any little spark of good will, and fan it—don't run over it. If you do, folks will just think you're dumb for not noticing.

If you be fair and don't cheat and don't be angry and don't try to take any position on someone while you're trying to get them to open up, when they do open up they'll see you standing there being fair and they'll have to love you, and they'll say, "Oh wow, man, were you trying to help me out all along? Far out!"

If it isn't cool, if you aren't able to get stoned, that's the time to say something.

If everything's cool, you ought to just *keep your mouth shut.*

Dharma is the fact that there is no Dharma, which is a Dharma. Dharma is truth to be taught. The Dharma you teach is that you are already equipped: you don't need any Dharma if you just pay attention to the here and now.

If you're just a little bit off, truth is complicated. If you're in it, it's beautiful and simple.

Some of the heaviest stuff that's been passed down for hundreds of thousands of years is that it seems to work better in the long run if we be good to each other. One of the forms of being good to each other that's been passed down is forgiveness.

Christ forgave them while they were doing it to him, even while it still hurt. It was a noble thing.

To forgive somebody, you've got to come and place your value in the real world, where the action is. You can't have all your value in your head, or your memory, or what you think you are, or how you think someone treated you. You can say, "Look, let's just write all that off. We know we really love one another," and just go on ahead.

Jesus said that if you come to pray and you have something against your brother, don't bother to pray right then—your mind won't be clear and can't do any good. Go back and find your brother and get straight with him. If you try and can't get straight, get two or three witnesses so that what was said may be established, and with those witnesses present, try to get straight. If that doesn't work, call on your brother in church, in front of all the congregation, and ask him to get straight with you in front of everyone. If he won't get straight with you then, you've done all you can and you don't have to worry about it any more. You can go on about your business.

Must I forgive my brother?
You must forgive your brother.
Seven times?
Nay. Seventy times seven.

The Bible

A blessing is what comes forth from your heart. If your heart is calm and full of love, you put out blessings that are calm and full of love.

There's no one so young or weak that his blessing is not strong. There's no one so crazy that his blessing is not strong. Everyone's blessing is strong. It's always worth it to try. Never underestimate your ability to help someone.

Put out your best love and your best good will, your deepest and most serious love all the time, because there's always someone who needs it.

The time you may notice compassion the most is by its sudden lack, like when someone says something tactless or thoughtless, and there's that sudden sick feeling when somebody has had something stepped on. What gets lost there is the ability to sustain compassion.

Compassion is the very bread of life. It's the assurance when we're with everybody that everything is cool. If somebody needs something, then there is the instrumenting of compassion, which is helping somebody to be comfortable so that they can become compassionate, too.

You can just change a situation from uncomfortable to comfortable immediately by how you individually and collectively be. It takes personal care, personal love, and immediate interpersonal responsibility to be sure that everybody is all right. You don't sign it off until you know that everybody is cool.

We each have to decide for ourselves what to do; how to do right and stay in balance. You don't want to be a hassle in the atmosphere all the time and you don't want to let things pass that shouldn't pass. About the most someone else can do for you is tell you that you have to do it for yourself.

Touch on the telepathic plane is compassion.
On the telepathic plane, we're all supposed to

*touch all the time. That's how we know
everything is cool, and everybody can relax*

True compassion is born of knowing your brother, knowing he's just the same as you are.

If there is not compassion, there is not enlightenment.

Love is an active verb. It's not an abstraction or a conceptual idea. You have to perform an action to show that it's really real.

Love is broadcast energy that actually physically helps sustain everyone exposed to it.

Love inter-penetrates. If I point a flash-light at you, and you point one at me, the lights don't stop each other. My light illuminates you; your light illuminates me, at the same time.

If you go out and just love everybody, then you're bound to get enough back. It happens to you as you get older—you meet more and more people that you fall in love with. You find yourself becoming naturally in love with lots of people, who you don't necessarily have to do a big Romeo and Juliet scene about. You can just relax and be warmed on the beauty of love.

The more love you put out, the more capable of loving you are. Love is infinite—and you have to love everybody. Even if someone does dumb and evil things, you have to understand where they're coming from, and love them anyway, even if you don't agree with their actions. Even if you have to *resist* their actions, you still have to love them. If you don't love them, there's no way you're ever going to help them. If you love them, it will help.

You shouldn't act on the basis of emotions other than love. You can be conditioned into other emotions too easily. So we prefer reason over emotions.

P.S. Love might tell you to do something unreasonable once in a while, and that's cool. You can't be reasonable all the time.

Don't be driven by your emotions—taste them to the fullest. Experience them; examine them. If somebody close to you has died and you're feeling grief, don't refuse to feel it. It'll just hang there, waiting to be felt, until sometime it'll catch you when you aren't looking. That's what a funeral service is for, to say, "Okay, let it hang out. We're all going to just let it go here. This is the place for it. It's okay. Bring your hankie. Let it go. Just let it happen." And if you *really* sit right on top of it and understand what it is that's bringing sorrow to you, and don't feel sorry for yourself—if you just stand right there, it will put you right out the top, and it will get you really high. Real grief has dignity.

That's with your own emotions. You don't want to mess with someone else's emotions, other than to say, "Hey, man, it ain't that bad," or "Take it easy," or "Can I help?" or sometimes you just take hold of someone and let them leak on you. And you maintain a little structure for both of you. Don't criticize it. Let it happen. And when they get done with it, you'll be there for them to hang on to. That's what compassion means. Feel it with them, so you share it. The magical part of it is that if you really share it, it really helps.

In other words the bodhisattva will rather share the sufferings of his fellowbeings in order to inspire and assist them on their way towards liberation than rest blissfully on the pedestal of his virtues, enjoying for himself the fruits of his good deeds thus the world is included in the process of liberation, and suffering is overcome by a compassion so allembracing that personal pain and grief lose all importance except as a further incentive for realizing the highest aim thus liberation from suffering has been transformed into liberation thru suffering. to put it differently: suffering is converted into a means of liberation, a purifying force hastening the process of spiritual maturing. consequently the ideal of monkhood as a means of escaping from the world is replaced by the ideal of bodhisattvahood which may be realized by householders and monks alike it has been said that the bodhisattva is one who renounces nirvana even if it is in his reach. as long as nirvana is conceived as a merely quietistic or negative ideal, namely as the individual liberation from suffering one may perhaps be able to speak of the bodhisattvas renunciation of such an ultimate state of nirvana but if we want to remain in the realm of the buddhas own definition of nirvana, according to which it consists in the overcoming of greed, hatred and ignorance (and thus having nothing to do with any kind of metaphysical speculation) then there can be no talk of a renunciation of nirvana on the part of the bodhisattva because that would be equivalent to an intentional retention of ignorance from which greed and hatred arise the bodhisattva does not renounce the highest knowledge but on the contrary for the sake of attaining perfect enlightenment he renounces a merely personal liberation from suffering ~ just as the buddha shakyamuni had done in his long career towards buddhahood ~ in order to let all fellowbeings partake in his own enlightenment and to kindle the spark of enlightment consciousness (bodhichitta) within them

lama govinda
maitreya three

65 97 98 82 22 45 99 19 81 28 89 59 52
41 100 29
30 42 95 6 25 1 27 26 3 85 15
96 55 76 2 54 53 86 18
47 56 40 4 93 84 77 24 52 7 23
88 49 13 44 5 75 78 83 60 33
8 87 79 37 11 92 43
38 94 39 9 80 10 91 16 70 20
31 14 51
61 67 5 32 46
63
21 12 25 17
35
64 68 69 62
74 75 36 73
65 32
5 18
2
14
22
15
8
15
101
25
8
16

If you were going to name and contain and count everything in the Universe, the first thing you would notice is that you need some kind of a counting tool, because obviously you would overamp your mind in trying to do a thing like that.

So you start counting off the things in the Universe. You start on your fingers. And then your toes. Use your elbows—say one elbow is one whole hand; an ear can be five hands of elbows—until pretty soon, you use that up.

So you get an adding machine. Pretty soon, you have every hole where a number could be, filled up with a nine. And you've used up the adding machine. You're still nowhere near all the stuff in the Universe.

So you keep on counting, and you say, "Okay. I'll start using other stuff to store the information on. I'll start using grains of sand." And you say, "All the grains of sand on the Pacific Ocean beach from Canada to Mexico." Then, "All the grains of sand of the river banks of the Ganges." And all the beaches of all the continents. You can use up the grains of sand and the pieces of gravel and all the dirt, and you're still counting and you ain't even getting there yet. Because all the stuff you've used up so far hasn't even gotten you into counting all the stuff on Earth.

And there's more stars than there are grains of sand on the Pacific Ocean beach from San Diego to Vancouver.

Every one of those stars has a possibility of planets and solar systems with river banks and beaches with grains of sand.

So you have to go from that level to the molecular level. You find that each grain of sand has so many molecules—and you still aren't getting there.

You want to contain this information about the Universe in something; but as you're using up the Universe to contain it, you reach a point where there is only one computer capable of containing the information, and that is *the thing itself*. It is the totality of everything in the entire Universe.

The Universe exists as held in the mind of God. The universe *is* the mind of God: more stars and galaxies than all the grains of sand on the Pacific Ocean beach. And within this mind there exist all of the connections and possibilities in the Universe.

Now the reason for this trip which we just went on is the idea, "What is God?" Some people insist that God is a person. They want to be able to relate to God, and they don't feel like they can relate to a rock, or half a cup of seawater. They want to have a *person* to relate to. But when you were using up all the grains of sand and all the molecules, you also used up all your brain cells and all the possibilities of interconnections among your brain cells.

In a way, your mind is a reflection of the mind of God. Because all these grains of sand and galaxies and stars, and this limitless space, was only understandable to you at all because inside each of our skulls is a model of the Universe.

A hologram is a new form of laser photography. You can set up an object and illuminate it with a laser, and capture the image on a special kind of film, and then you can project that image with laser light through that piece of film, like showing a movie. But it does a slightly different thing. In a hologram, you can look at, say, a coffee can, with writing on it. And around the bottom of the coffee can is a little line of print that tells you what it weighs and where it was made. You can read that across the front of the coffee can, and when you get done there you can walk over a little ways and see the coffee can from another view, and you can continue reading the sentence. It's a three hundred and sixty degree picture.

Well, if you have a negative for a hologram and you tear off a little corner of it and project through that little corner, you don't see a little corner of the picture: you see the *whole picture*.

That's the way your mind relates to the mind of God. You can just fall through that little picture, out into limitless galaxies of space and stars. It's *all* in there.

All you have to do to meet God is to understand that you are a corner of it. God is intelligent. And the person, person-ness and personality of the godhead is *you*. God exists mentally perceptible to us as the sense of eye/I-ness—the sense of identity wherever it occurs in the Universe.

It's like a light inside you. If you put too many filters on it, not much light gets out. You just have to *let go of assuming that you're the whole picture, and realize that there **is** a whole picture.*

One of the most difficult things to do is to recognize the existence of God as the totality of the Universe.

Some people think I'm trying to do away with God when I'm not into the curly-bearded man in the white suit. But I feel like that's a very *limiting* idea of God. If there is anything that God is, it is not limited.

I was talking with someone and he said, "Why is a cow a cow? What's the right name of anything? We call stuff by names. How do we know what God's name for it is? Maybe he's got numbers." And I told him he had just stumbled onto the edge of Zen. Part of Zen is that when you look at someone or something or anything, you see what it is. Not the name of it, or what you previously knew about it, or your preconceptions. But you see what is. And it has no name. *It is its own name.* A name is only a signal. The only reality a name has is a piece of noise.

You are born. The first question you ask, and the next question, and the next one for about the next seventy-five to a hundred and ten years is, "What is it?"

And people say, "It's the sky." "It's your diaper." "It's your Aunt Sally." "It's your nose." "Don't touch that—it's hot." "Leave it alone, it's not yours." All that stuff is what it's *for*. What it *is,* is God.

"What's this thing with the rubber end on it I'm sticking in my mouth?" *"It's God."* "What are these things I'm putting on my feet?" *"It's God."* That's a little inconvenient. You need a little differentiation to tell your nursing bottle from your galoshes. But don't get caught up in the differentiation and think that it means anything at all, other than a little matter of convenience.

Everything you do is right here in front of God and everybody. There isn't anywhere you can go. God is also out behind the barn, and in your deepest heart of hearts. God is not only every grain of sand and every massive star, but every plane and level of existence, material and immaterial, thought of or as yet unthought of; every level of vibration; every realm of imagination, every possibility—is all God.

Even in the back of your mind, where you sometimes think uncharitable things about people because you don't think anybody is listening—is God, sitting there listening.

What is that thing that observes that?

You want to find God? Spend just a couple of seconds. Look around inside your head for God. Just look around inside your head for God. Can you find him? You having trouble finding him? *Who is looking?*

That's who is looking.

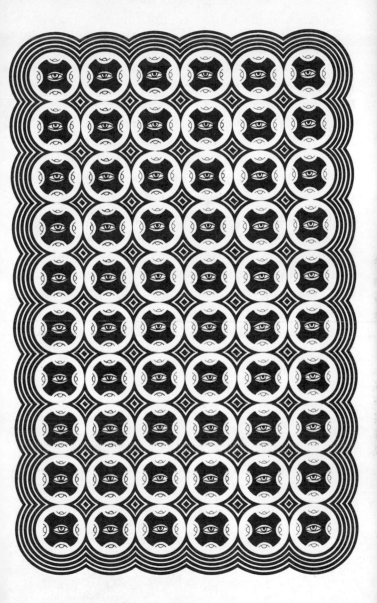

There's a saint who said, "It is easier to live a good life than it is to think good thoughts." We have the gift of intelligence and consciousness to a level where it's a controversy whether we're the highest of the apes or the lowest of the angels. But a part of us is ape. Ape thoughts are going to come up now and then, and you can't think you're a bad person or anything like that. Don't get strung out about your thoughts. You don't have to do what you think. Your thoughts are like a drawing board. Draw better stuff. Don't worry about it. Be nice. If you *be* nice, it will be easier to *think* nice, because you won't be using that other stuff and it will wither away from not being used.

Integrity is something you have to work at every day; it isn't something you naturally have forever. I know a day doesn't go by for me that I don't have to think, "I have *got* to get it together."

A good man transcends his discipline. If he's a good man, he'll transmit goodness out of his heart.

Do what you know is right. Look at a situation and, without being attached, decide what is right and do it. Never mind your head trips. Decide what is right and do it. When you learn how to do that, it's a great refuge and a great peace.

You can make a difference in *anything* if you try hard enough. You have to learn how to put out effort *psychically*. Physically, if you try to pick up something that's heavier than you thought, you go back and collect yourself a little more and you try again, and maybe you still can't, and you really collect yourself and you just pour your whole thing into it, and it'll budge. You have to learn how to do that *psychically*. You have to learn how to put out the kind of effort as if you were going to press two hundred pounds.

You have to exercise your muscles by doing stuff that's hard to do. It's just like anything else—you don't build yourself into a champion weight lifter by trying to move around styrofoam. You have to pump a little iron. If you're going to build your psychic muscle, you have to do stuff that's hard to do.

If your good sense tells you that you're self-indulgent to ask for a second piece of cake, and part of you wants it, you can say, "No, it's a matter of principle. I won't do it." Every time you make a decision like that, you build yourself and strengthen yourself, so that when you want to be more aware, you can just put out your attention like a search light.

Most of us are so conditioned and so sloppy of mind and handle our minds in such habitual fashions as to be almost sleepwalking; *just almost sleepwalking* from our normal cultural upbringing.

In Zen, the idea of sitting is not that sitting is going to get you enlightened. The idea is that you're so spaced that you've got to learn to do something right, and that you can start with sitting because it seems pretty simple.

So the first thing is you learn to sit. It takes me about fifteen minutes to gather my head from all the little trips that are going on and all the things I'm thinking about—all the distractions—and get myself gathered together and in one place—get myself *sat*. Then you might wonder what are you supposed to do once you get sat: what is meditation in that sense?

They say, "sitting is enlightenment." You aren't sitting there expecting something. You're not waiting for an effect to happen. But if you ever get your head clean and clear, then the mind and the body go under natural automatic pilot, which is a perfectly clean machine, and you are healed. Just to sit there and shut up is healing to your sanity and to your body—to your whole mind.

There are some tricks of the trade for doing that. People have things that they're worried about come into their mind and bother them. Things are going to bubble up out of your consciousness, and pop into your mind while you're sitting, and you have to do something about them. You might have to go find somebody and get cool with them, in order for that voice to shut up in your head. If you're in a meditation and it's not appropriate to get up and go look somebody up right then, you can make a firm decision and a firm promise to yourself that next time you get a chance you're going to find that person and you're going to get straight.

That will usually free you enough on that question, if you trust yourself enough to believe yourself when you tell yourself something like that. If you've been pretty spacey and loose, you may say, "Yeah, yeah, yeah. You just say you will." But get the house cleaned up, get all the beds made up here in your head. Then you aren't doing anything with your head; you're just letting it sit there in its perfect state.

Here's one trick you can do for a start. If your mind is tending to wander and think about a lot of stuff, follow your breath in, and follow it out. Don't necessarily try to breathe evenly, but count the first in-breath as one, the next as two, and continue counting until you get up to ten; and when you get to ten, come back down—nine, eight, seven, six, and back down to one again. That's twenty breaths. Well, it may take you practicing for weeks to get yourself to where you can go through twenty breaths without spacing out and finding yourself out into "fifteen, sixteen, seventeen," or lost in various directions: "Oh! I remember now, I was counting my breaths."

But when you get your attention to where you can do that pretty reliably, then you can get purer. You can let go of the numbers and become less conceptual. You can just follow your breath, in and out, in and out, very quietly. Don't make a fuss. You don't have to do anything about it, but just leave your attention there because it gives your mind something to do.

That gets you to a pretty pure place, but there's a purer place past that. In the Japanese tradition they call it *shikan-taza,* which is the highest form of meditation. You can let your mind be perfectly empty and not have to concentrate on your breath. Your breath is doing it on automatic pilot. You just let your mind be perfectly quiet. If you can reach that state, you can get very clean and very pure and get yourself very stoned.

I love to meditate outside because you can put your attention in one or another sense, and if the dogs are running out in front and distracting you, or something like that, you can close your eyes and put your attention into your hearing, and listen to the birds, and the wind, which have no ego in them at all. They're very pure sounds. It will not put you on a trip to listen to the birds. And if you listen to them very carefully, your consciousness will rise and rise and rise, to a point where you won't be listening to the birds anymore. You'll just be experiencing everything—the wind, the birds, sitting here, us together, feeling our minds all at once, feeling everything happen.

Sometimes in the meditative state you kind of poke out through the top and you forget everything for a while, but basically the meditative state is very aware and very alert and very together, just completely at rest. If someone should walk up and whisper your name from twenty feet away, you should just be right there. You should not have to go through a bunch of adjustments to know what's going on around you. You should be very clear and very together; you should be in perfect condition.

They say that if you are paying complete attention to what it is you are doing, you are in the footsteps of the Buddha. What that means is that you are completely engrossed in the task that you are doing, be it sitting zazen, playing music, driving a car, planting tomatoes, whatever it is that you are doing. If you are not paying attention to yourself, you aren't thinking about how good a job you are doing. You are in a pure state, a meditative state. You are being healed all the time you're there.

If you find that your mind is turning back on itself and thinking about itself all the time, that mainly means that you are not working hard enough or what you are doing is too easy and too far below your capabilities. You ought to be trying harder, because if you've got any left over to turn around and look back with, it's too easy. Try something harder. Try to integrate more stuff. Take on a heavier load, because when you are fully loaded and fully busy, you won't be self-conscious. You'll just be scratching to keep it together, and that's a pretty healthy condition.

The pure state has no content. It is what it is. In Zen they talk about perfection-ness—the ISness. Not even "Just is," you know. The "just" is unnecessary. It's not even "Only is;"

Sometimes when the wind blows I can feel it blowing through us like we were a field of wheat. I can feel the wind in everybody's hair besides mine, and I know that we're not really different from the wheat. We tend to encase our roots in a pair of shoes rather than just stick them down in the dirt, but we aren't really that different.

The wind blows by and our season passes, too, just like the wheat season passes. We'd better do it while we're ripe, before our season passes.

If you find a problem in the Universe, instead of saying, "Why isn't somebody watching this?" you have to notice that you are the one who saw it. You are God's eyes on the scene. If you say, "Why didn't somebody take care of this?" and walk away, you've just checked out on your obligation to be God's eyes on the scene.

If we really are all One, and we really are telepathic, then we are our brother's keeper, and it really does matter what we do. How we be makes a difference for how it is for everyone in the world.

There is a certain religious view that says being on earth is like being on a huge circle-the-planet airplane; that God is the pilot and that the airline has certain obligations to you as passenger—that all you have to do is settle back and say, "Thank you for all of this." But it ain't like that at all.

You're not a paying passenger on the airline. You're a hippie stowaway, and you ain't got bread to pay your passage. You need to work. This is a spaceship with all crew and no passengers. It only works right if all concerned are trying as hard as they can. Man and God are not separate—if man lays back, then part of God is laying back, and you cannot expect the best of all possible universes. Being enlightened is taking conscious part in helping God with His Universe, saying, "Well, I'd better do what I can to try to make things stretch. It seems like some folks are having trouble making things stretch." If you really understand the situation, you'd like to help.

Two of the Precepts of the Gurus, in Tibetan Yoga, are that you must be like a man who has been bitten by a snake and knows he has not a moment to lose; and that you must be like a man who has awakened to find that his horse has been stolen and it is too late to lock the door, and there is no hurry.

No matter how hard you blow your mind, no matter how much white light you have seen, no matter what unendurable ecstasies of power and knowledge you have gone through, what it all comes down to is that we are all One, and what are you going to do about it? With infinite patience, not moving so fast as to alienate anyone, *carefully and gently let out the news.*

Everyone should be figuring out what they can really do; what they can *really* handle. We have so much to do; we need so much help and so much cooperation and so many people to step out and take responsibility . . . *to step out into it.*

I don't think you just pack it in and be a hermit forever. If you retreat, you do it until you learn something and then you come back out and sock it to the world—*give them some.*

You can't let your search for God make you turn your back on man; helping man is a good place to start your search for God.

It's hard for people to be spiritual who are hungry. It's difficult to talk about Spirit to an empty belly—just irrelevant. You have to feed them something—get them high on beans if they don't have anything else—and create the conditions where Spirit can grow and flower.

God is eternal, infinite, and inexhaustible; you don't have to be afraid and slow down like you do in the material plane.

In the material plane, there is diminishing returns and entropy and that sort of thing, but in the spiritual plane it's go for broke all the time.

Start a large project—like saving the world. Keeps you busy. Guaranteed for a lifetime. That's what the Vow of the Bodhisattva is about:

The deluding passions are inexhaustible.
  I vow to extinguish them all.
Sentient beings are numberless.
  I vow to save them all.
The truth is impossible to expound.
  I vow to expound it.
The way of the Buddha is unattainable.
  I vow to attain it.

If you get into high levels of consciousness, you can become compassionate with your brother. You can feel the man next to you or the lady or the child or the dog or the tree or whatever next to you, you can feel them, and if you get pretty stoned, you can feel everybody in the room. You can get stoneder and you can feel everybody in the house. You can get stoneder and you can feel everybody on the block. You can get high and you can feel everybody in town, and if you get higher, you can feel everybody in the country. And if you get a little higher, you can feel everybody in the world. You can feel them all.

That's where the catch is. When you can find yourself feeling everybody in the world, you suddenly notice that about a third of your brothers and sisters are starving. About a billion people are starving on this planet, and you are no better than those folks are. It is purely a geographical accident.

There is only one way you can go to that level and be able to stand it. That is to know in your heart of hearts that you're doing everything you possibly can to help out.

If you had a bucketful of amoebas, and one of them died and another one divided, so there were just as many of them, wouldn't we call it the same bucket of amoebas? Well, here we are. The same bucket. We as a bucket know things that we don't know as individuals—as an individual, we might even be one that was just replaced last week. That's what is meant by "racial memory" and the "collective unconscious;" it's the memory of that bucket of amoebas. Among the highest things man does is to try to identify himself not as himself—who may have been an amoeba that was replaced last week—but with the whole bucket. And see what does the whole bucket know.

Enlightenment is not so much making it to the

it's more like getting off

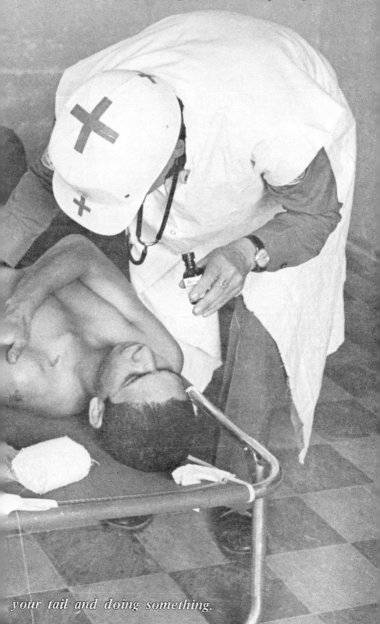

never-never land through the secret passageway—

your tail and doing something.

esus was a revolutionary. Otherwise, they never would have bothered to nail him up, because he wouldn't have been dangerous to Caesar. Being spiritual is not to meditate until you blow the top of your brain out, and it's not to go off and take that one big trip on the mountaintop by yourself. It is to realize, once you know we're all One, that your energy has to be at the service of mankind. Every one of those spiritual teachers who ever made that crossing—Saint Francis, Mohammed, Jesus, Buddha, Krishna—came back and said, "Hey! We're all One!"

We all know that now. We've been knowing that for a while. What do you do if you know that we're all One? How do you live?

There is a necessity for revolution. A revolution is not about hurting people; a revolution is about making changes. The best way to do that is to live your life right—massively—and do it clean and good and obviously out in front for people to look at. And if you don't violate the people's trust, the people will back you up.

Trucker's Prayer

O Lord give me strength to make this run
For US currency and not for fun
Please help me not to have a flat
No engine trouble — or likes of that
Help me pass the scale and I.C.C.
Make the J.P.'s let me go free
Keep the Sunday drivers out of my way
And women drivers too I pray
And when I sleep in this stinking cab
Let me wake where there is fine eggs to grab
Make the coffee strong and the women weak
And the waitress girls and not some freak
Make the highways better, the gas and fuel cheaper
And on my next run, Lord help me get a sleeper
If you'll do this O Lord and with
a little luck
I keep right on drivin
A damm old truck

What's truly revolutionary is growing your own food instead of supporting the profit system. It's revolutionary to deliver your own babies instead of paying a thousand dollars a head to profit-oriented hospitals and doctors. It's revolutionary to get the knowledge out of college and make it so you don't have to sell your soul to learn something. It's revolutionary to learn how to fix stuff, rather than junk it or take it in to be replaced.

You can learn how to take care of yourself. And that's revolutionary, because if you want any independence, it comes with taking care of yourself.

Learn how to make a living for yourself and some other people—get strong enough to take care of somebody besides yourself. Don't get caught doing something dumb. Don't get caught in a job that will be phased out when the money gets tough.

The illusion of separateness is preyed upon by "Buy the fastest Corvette on the block so you'll be different;" "Wear these kinds of clothes so you'll be different;" "Comb your hair this way . . ." The society is pushing us to a level of individuality that's neurotic. It makes it possible for us to watch somebody else get hurt and be able to disassociate it enough to say, "Well, it's not my business," and walk away from it.

It IS your business.

If you raise your head up out of the level of self-interest, and look at the whole world like that, you start seeing what's really important.

Darwin said that competition is what causes the species to evolve, and that theory was taken over by businessmen as a justification for power politics and power economics. But at the same time that Darwin published, a fellow named Kropotkin also published, and everything that he published says that *cooperation* is how animals make it. He points out that there aren't any more sabre-toothed tigers, but the cockroach has lived unchanged for a hundred and thirty-six million years.

If the dirt in a can of worms gets dry, the worms all crawl up close together to share what moisture they have. It seems that if a can of worms can cooperate when the earth gets dry, mankind ought to learn to cooperate too.

If you're going to say we're all One, let's give up competition at that level of food and life and death and housing, and things like that.

Social position is relative. It's higher than something else, lower than something else. Position is a space/time phenomenon. The thing about God-realization is that there is no space or time on that plane. On the material plane, everybody can't be in the same place at the same time because there's only so much room, but on that other plane, everyone can be in the same place at the same time. That is the level where, by its nature, by the topology and geometry of that plane, there is no necessity for competition.

There was this barrel out in the middle of a field, and these two little kids came over and were hanging around with this barrel. One of them was on one side pushing, and one was on the other side, pushing, and they were playing with it. Then one of them walked around to the other side and they both gave a heave together, and it moved. They both looked at each other and said, "Mm-hm." And they learned cooperation. They rolled that barrel across the field, and stirred up so much juice by that cooperation that all the five- and six-year-old kids came over and took it away from them because it was such a good deal.

I really believe that religion is the most non-violent and least abrasive structure, particularly compared to a political one. A political structure has two functions for folks: to gain power within the hierarchy; and to do battle against opposite political parties. There are two directions of hassle going on in a political party from the start, before you even get into how the people get along. Politics is a matter of power confrontation—winner take all. Spirit says that no one is expendable—that everyone must be accounted for, even if it slows the thing down.

A politically based equality says that man is equal at the lowest common denominator. A religiously based equality says that man is equal at the highest common denominator. Through God, we partake of our real equality.

Holy
Spirit
is life-
force. Just
to perceive it
is to be blessed.
To perceive it and
know what it is, is to be
doubly blessed. And to perceive it, and know what it is,
and continue to be a channel to

bring more of it into the world for
everybody to use is to be thrice
blessed: it creates us all
happier and stronger and
more alive in the here
and now,   in   the
material   world
and
on.

"Make us worthy, Lord, to serve our brothers and sisters throughout the world who live and die in hunger and poverty. Give them through our hands this day their daily bread and by our understanding peace, give them joy."

—Mother Teresa

Large, widespread knowledge about the reality of Spirit is proof of the presence of redemption on the planet at this time.

If you know that Spirit and energy determine matter, not that matter determines Spirit and energy—then you can do things that make a difference in the world.

It's so good for anybody to help out mankind that if you really do it, you'll get backed up, your credit rating will be good. You'll get helped out in every imaginable way if you will step out and try to help mankind, because that is so valuable.

Jesus said that His relationship with the twelve apostles was a model of the church to come. You can look at their relationship and see that He was very telepathic with them. He says things like, if you're busted in a small town, don't worry about what to say to the judge. Words will be put in your mouth when the time comes for you to speak. Or, words that have been whispered in your ear, shout from the rooftops. He also said, "I am the vine, and you are the branches;" "I am the tree and you are the limbs;" "I am the head and you are the body." *Christ is a consciousness, and we are His body; and his presence can be manifested on earth through us, any time we are heavy enough and believe it enough, and get it together enough to do it.*

In Judaism, they say that when the ills of man become intolerable and just men ask God for a Messiah, the Messiah will come. I believe that this generation can do it, but the question is *do they do it?* A person can go to a spiritual plane and see how it should be — and then he has his free will choice about whether to bring that about. So that's the question we all have to answer, each individual in his own heart:

Do we, of our own free will, bring about the Kingdom of God on earth as it is in Heaven?

Being born into this world gives you the right to attempt to change it. It's just a question of being very wise and very kind and very careful about what you do to folks and what you advocate. Some folks say that you can't know good and evil anyway, and that in a million years nobody will know the difference; and that if you backed off to the highest, most universal point of view, it seems that there's nothing you can do about it; and they talk about how you can't really hurt anyone because we're all part of God anyway, so what you do doesn't really matter because God is going to do His thing. But there's a specific teaching in the Bible that gives you the key to understanding that. It says, *He marks the sparrow's fall.* Even if continents are starving and a million people are being born every day, *He marks the sparrow's fall.* It matters what you do and how you be. Some folks say, "It's only little old me, it doesn't matter what I do." *Every way you be matters.*

You have to realize that you are responsible for where you are at and for where your life is at. How you are is the result of your past decisions; and if you don't like the way you are, you can, with a little effort of will, change your decisions for awhile and you will change into being another way.

You have to do it inside yourself: a good moral structure imposed from the outside is totalitarianism. If you do it, you'll hook in with other folks doing it. You have to make interior decisions when nobody's looking: all by yourself, in your head, take full responsibility for what you are about to do: and do the best you can.

After you do it awhile you'll begin to expect it of yourself.

Your *self-concept* is one of the strongest barriers to change, because it tends to lock you up and make you say things like, "Well, I'm a brave man. I always react brave." What if the right thing to do is to just shut up and back down? If that's the only appropriate thing to do, are you going to be bound? Are you going to be so you can't do it because your self-concept says you have to react in a brave fashion?

You have to be a free enough soul to change your behavior in such a way as to help folks out without making any judgments about them. Don't have any self-concepts about what you might do in a given situation: you have to be completely free to do whatever's right at that time.

A situation cannot change without a variable. Remember that little plastic game that has fifteen squares in it, and sixteen spaces, and you can slide the squares around? Well, if it wasn't for that empty square, you couldn't do anything. Right? Everything would be locked up. That space is the variable in the situation. All change possible in the situation is because of that empty square.

If you be an empty square, empty of desires, empty of prejudices, empty of heavy opinions, empty of being really attached to how it comes out—if you be an empty square, you can be the variable in the situation, and the whole thing can change.

If you can change, you can do anything.

If you change yourself, you change the world.

To change yourself, you have to see the necessity for it, and you have to put out the energy to do it. If you think you're already cool, then you won't get up any energy to bother to try to change.

This is not to say that you have to think of yourself as imperfect, or the world as imperfect. Rather, you realize that change *is*; that everything changes, and that we're not changing in the sense of running away from something, but changing *toward something*.

You have to be willing to change and to grow. There's nobody so bad off they can't, and nobody so cool they don't need to.

In one of my psychedelic experiences, I was in a cocoon picking my way out, and I kicked my way out of the cocoon. When I got out, I looked around and there were all these cocoons all spread out on the cocoon tray. Some of them were lying still and some of them were wiggling. Some of them had an arm sticking out; some were fighting their way out. I leaned back and I looked up, and I saw this giant hooded figure seated on a star, looking down at the cocoon tray, and then it was *me* up there looking down at the cocoon tray. "Far out," I thought, "Far out."

One way you can really demonstrate the existence of Spirit, the existence of Mind, is to change visibly so everybody who knows you sees you change. Most people think that people are slow to change; and if somebody actually *changes,* people are impressed.

If you find out you're wrong, give up.

Change doesn't mean being different than you really are. If you think that being nice is being different than you really are, it's going to keep you hanging on the edge of nutty because denying who you really are gets you crazy. Who you *really* are wants out.

We believe that everybody is basically good. They may have selfish ways, but basically they're good. We're all perfect when we're born, and we pick up bad habits as we go along.

So if somebody tells you to change in some way, don't be afraid you're going to lose *you*, because you aren't. You can't lose you. There are people who have run very fast many miles, trying to lose themselves, and been unable to do it. So don't worry about losing you. It's okay to change. You can't change the real part, because the real part's the God part and it doesn't change.

You are stone naked when you meet God. You haven't got on a grey flannel suit or a burnoose or a loin cloth or anything. It doesn't matter what language you speak, because He takes it right out of your mind before you put it into a language.

O my friends, have no fixed abode inside or outside, and your conduct will be perfectly free and unfettered. Take away your attachment and your walk will know no obstruction whatever.

— Buddhist scriptures

The object of most Zen practice or yoga is to become deconditioned. Unconditioned man is essentially good and essentially smart.

Man's free will is his Holy Gift from God. Insofar as we have free will, we have a piece of God's spirit. A lot of the teachings about behavior from the Holy books are about ways to attain and to give free will.

But a conditioned reflex bypasses people's free will — it bypasses the brain's reasoning functions. Every time you're conditioned over a particular issue, it means that a particular circuit in your mind is used up. You can't release that circuit to use it for anything else — it's a busy signal on that line. If you have enough of those, it starts cutting into your intelligence, your memory, your efficiency, and how well you can make it. It uses you up until, for some folks, there is hardly enough to cope.

To the extent that you're sane and free and of free mind and whole heart, you have more and more free will. There is an absolute potential of free will, because that comes from God. You may be pretty conditioned in any given moment, but you *can have free will*.

You can condition folks by conditioned behavior that you are unaware of. If someone's mother always said, "That's nice," for what he did, he could learn that as conditioned response behavior, and transmit that to his children. That's one of the inner meanings of the Biblical phrase, "The sins of the fathers shall be visited on the sons, yea unto the third generation."

So you have a duty, in your relationship with everyone, to be scrupulously honest, and to try not to condition someone to get what you want. It's okay to say, "Can I have that?" But it is not okay to condition someone to give it to you.

Pay attention all the time.
Pay attention all the time.
What can you do to get unconditioned?
Pay attention all the time.
Don't take anything for granted.
Pay attention all the time.

Here's the thing about conditioning: If it makes you mad, it's doing it to you.

To the extent that we are affected by praise and blame, we all condition each other all the time whether we know it or not.

Praise and blame is as if, instead of developing your own sense of what time it is, you always have to ask somebody else what time it is; you never keep track yourself, and you don't have a watch and you wouldn't have one, but you all the time ask other people what time it is. If you want to be free of praise and blame, carry your own watch, and then you *know* what time it is, and you don't have to ask anybody.

Another way to describe it is *affectionate detachment:* not caring what people say about you. You can't be steered by what people say about you.

If you've done something dumb, there is nothing you can do in your head to undo it. If somebody has stepped on your ego in a way that is hard for you to forget, there is nothing you can do in your head to repair that. Cut loose. Don't past-trip.

When you notice you're on a trip, that's God who notices. If you can avoid being embarrassed and squirming, dig who caught you!

Love is a free will act. You can love someone because you want to, because it's right. You can do it on purpose, as a matter of decision. If you think you fall in love by accident or get angry by accident, you are like a ship with no rudder, banging around from event to event that attracts your attention; and you don't get smarter. But if you understand that you *can* love on purpose and you *can* be not angry on purpose, then you can use free will.

If you love any one kind of people better than another kind, then you're not being fair and you're conditioning folks. You can't just love Protestants or Catholics or Jews or men or women or children or animals. Or trees. Or cute ladies. Or strong men. People are different, but they aren't *that* different. You have to love everybody.

You need to decondition yourself so you can go back to being fresh and clean like a brand new baby. Just take it like it comes to you the first time, and respond. Clean in, clean out. Clean in, clean out.

In the Indian spiritual disciplines, *prana* is spiritual energy, and they say that when you're meditating, you're collecting *prana*. The more you collect, the stoneder you get. Each one of us is an electro-chemical organism with a field around us, which the Hindus call the aura. If two people stand together, their auras interpenetrate and there is a resultant aura that has two flavors—from the two people. With a group of people, we have a group aura, which is both strengthened and flavored by each person's field.

Even though that is a pool which we create, we are also nourished from that pool. If we put too much garbage into it, we begin to get a little garbage back out of it. If we put too much anger, fear, violence, lust, and greed into it, it begins to flavor it so strongly that the flavor is a little paranoid, a little scared on the lower levels. On the higher levels,

God is eternal, and contains all the changes. That pool contains the record of all mankind, but it changes from generation to generation. There are periods of history when mankind has done better than he's doing right now. There were times when there was peace in China for hundreds of years. They say that at one time a beautiful virgin with a sack of gold could ride across China without a guard, and nobody would bother her. So we could be doing better.

What can you do to help? You can change yourself, so you don't add any more of that flavor to the soup. That's the first thing you can do. Then, if you have it to where you're putting out pretty good stuff, maybe you can absorb a little from somebody else. If somebody comes by you who's angry, for example, you can absorb it, reason with them, help them out, maybe bring them out of it. And that is a service to mankind: not just to the person you help out, but to mankind.

If you find yourself getting angry, you can take that as a signal that there's something you want or don't want. Find out what it is. That's the time to look back inside yourself and say, "Why does that make me angry? I think I'm going to lose something." Lao Tsu says, "If you feel deflated, maybe you were inflated."

Anger is also a response to being scared. Something scares you and you be angry to back it off. It's very basic, almost instinctive; but we have to rise above that, because anger is psychic violence.

If someone is angry at you, you have to be calm and unthreatened enough to be unthreatening; and brave enough that you're not frightened by it.

You can be strong enough to not panic if everybody else around you is panicking. If you can do that, you can quell a panic so it doesn't happen. You can be so strong that somebody can come to you afraid, and have to quit being afraid, because of your psychic strength. .

Their fear will not make you afraid; your non-fear will make them calm.

Make it so you don't have any stake. You aren't trying to get rich, so you won't be mad if somebody gets the money. You won't be mad if somebody takes the girl you were going to date. You can *pre-decide* all that stuff, and you can unload your circuits. Then, when you go into a situation where there's a lot of heavy emotion, even if you feel it running through you, you don't have to act on it. You don't have to assume it's yours; it's more like being in a room with someone, breathing the same air. You're going to share some of it, whatever is going on. But you don't have to make your decisions on the basis of it.

You can sit quietly until you see the part of your mind that makes decisions. You can isolate your free will. You can see your thought processes go by. You see your desires. You might think, "Somebody did this to me, and I didn't like it," or something like that. But you can isolate your fair witness. Then, when you're in a heavy situation, make all your decisions from the fair witness.

There's a certain feeling of dissatisfaction that's similar to hunger, or loss. It's an uncomfortable feeling. It's the way you feel when you don't get what you want. If you are going to grow to any appreciable level, you are going to have to experience that feeling.

> Once there was a great, great king. He called his wise man and said, "I would like you to give me a magic statement: a spell that will always be true, and will have the magical power of making me happy when I'm sad, and making me sad when I'm happy." His wise man came back to him and gave him a little ring, and inscribed inside the ring was the magic spell. It said, **"This too shall pass away."**
> —*Old Sufi Tale*

Attachments are pieces of you that have become rigid and are no longer flexible. When you meet with a new situation, all of you can respond to it except the attachments.

The advantage of non-attachment is that you get to do what you think is right *all the time*. Being unattached keeps the vibrations steady and level—what you think is right when you're non-attached has a steady, level vibration. Reality can only change so much, gracefully, from frame to frame.

There's a kind of freedom I'm trying to bring you. I think the only freedom man has comes through responsibility. If you become responsible, you become able to act; and if you can act, you're free. Freedom comes with sanity, because if you're sane you can figure out what to do, and you can use your free will.

I really want people to understand that freedom comes with responsibility. There's no way I can give you freedom, because if I give it to you, it isn't free. So if you want any freedom, you're just going to have to get it yourself.

I like to hang out with brand new babies that are just born, because I can let go and feel a lot of peace. But as soon as I get peaceful, I find that what I have to do is get up and go back out and start taking care of business again, because there's a lot of folks that still need help, and we can't rest yet.

You're supposed to be grooving

as hard as you can all the time.

There is an ongoing search for the Holy.
Once you've had a taste of it, you have to have
some more of it, and get closer to it.

We have a religion that was put together while we were under intense revelation. The revelations lasted long enough that we could talk about them in between the times they were going on and we could say, "Did you see that happen?" so we learned a bunch of stuff. We didn't know what it was and then we studied what we'd learned and we found out it was religion.

When I had a real religious experience, it blew my mind completely. I saw how the Universe works, I saw the nature of karma and good and evil, positive and negative, and yang and yin. I saw what were Christs and Buddhas and Bodhisattvas and demons and devils, and I understood what all that was and how it all worked. I could do it in religious terms or philosophical terms or mathematical terms and it all worked, and it all came out in the same answers. It said we were all One and that you can know truth; that we, by the way we be, change and create the Universe as we come to it: that we create our karma as it comes to us; that cause and effect on the spiritual plane is just the same as cause and effect on any other plane.

I saw that society was a colloid solution and that if you tried to push it too fast it would tend to make the colloid get rigid. If you pushed it at just the right speed, the colloid would be fluid and malleable and you could actually move large pieces of society fairly easily as long as you didn't override the nature of the colloid; that it was a matter of agreement, and that if you had agreement, then, as it says in the Bible, "If two of you agree as touching anything, it shall be done." I saw all that stuff and it changed my life and I quit being the way I was being before; I started being a whole new different way.

I saw how everything worked. I saw that one person, if he was patient enough and if he really took the time, could change the world.

We're supposed to treat each other like brothers and sisters. The whole of the law shall be to love God with all your heart and soul and mind and strength, and love your neighbor as yourself. If you abide by these, you need no other law. That's what Jesus said — Love God. Love each other.

Grace. That's what Christ brings.

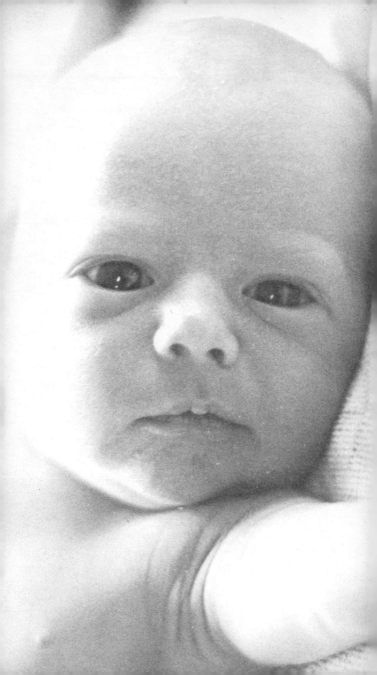

What is going to carry us through is faith and love and good principles. Faith that there are such things as love and good principles, and the nerve to try to use them and carry them out.

We should ask for the sake of all mankind that there be peace and that there be understanding and that God's grace come onto us to help us get this planet together, because this planet needs to get together.